UNTIL NEXT

BY

LORI JOHNSON

Copyright © *Lori Johnson,* 2024
All Rights Reserved

This book is subject to the condition that no part of this book is to be reproduced, transmitted in any form or means, electronic or mechanical, stored in a retrieval system, photocopied, recorded, scanned, or otherwise. Any of these actions require the proper written permission of the author.

TABLE OF CONTENTS

Dedication 3

Acknowledgements 4

Introduction 8

Chapter One Contradiction 1

Chapter Two Surprise 6

Chapter Three Preparation 10

Chapter Four Serenity 15

Chapter Five The Reality 24

Chapter Six Back to Normal… Nothing is Normal 34

Chapter Seven The Roller Coaster Ride That Is Grief ... 41

Chapter Eight Ain't No Mountain High Enough 46

Chapter Nine The Collective Consciousness 50

Chapter Ten Love, Forgiveness, Gratitude, Abundance 56

Chapter Eleven What do we do now? 61

Chapter Twelve Closure 65

Chapter Thirteen The Gift 69

Epilogue 71

Dedication

I dedicate this book to my son Robert William Johnson, who was born an angel.

Robert (Robbie) was born on July 10th, 1990.

Robbie was loved as much in the brief moments of life as he would have been if he had lived to be one hundred years old.

We loved the little boy who grew inside me, and we could not wait to meet him.

While he was in utero, we began to learn his personality, likes and dislikes, sleep habits, wake times, exercise routines, and so many other things.

We anticipated the arrival of this little boy and could not wait to watch him live his life and become the person he was meant to be.

I dedicate this book to my first husband and Robbie's dad, Steven Reid Johnson. Reid passed away on September 15th, 2018. He is in heaven with his son, which is the most comforting thought.

I, most importantly, dedicate this book to all the parents who have experienced the death of a baby.

To love a child you never got to know or only knew for a very short time in this reality is a profound experience that is still misunderstood.

I truly hope this book can illuminate the deep loss and contradictory emotions of a loss like no other.

Acknowledgements

I want to start this acknowledgement section by saying that being ready to write took time and effort.

Obviously, the years in between my son's death and now is a long time. However, it has been the last two and a half years that gave me all that I needed to be ready to illuminate light on my story.

One day, two years ago or so, my neighbour, Trisha Cuthbertson, Owner of Trisha's More than Just Cards, invited me to a Women's Business Networking group meeting. I thought, why not. You never know who you might meet.

On our way there, I asked her if she knew anyone who supported new business wannabes in writing business plans. Of course, she did, as she is well-connected in our community. Little did we know that Trisha's referral would change everything for me. Thank you, Trisha. I will always be grateful for the introductions.

Her referrals were to Karen Collacutt, Founder of 6-Figure Profit Surge for Coaches and Consultants, Karen Collacutt International Inc. and Karen Kessler, Speaker, Trainer, Author, and Co-Founder of Big Blue Door. This introduction changed my life.

I started by working with these fantastic women on a course design.

This led me to take many more of their courses. I wanted more of their brilliance. The Karens also offered a group for entrepreneurs, The Big Blue Door, where I met many more amazing women and men pursuing their dreams.

I am so glad I took Trisha up on the invite to the networking meeting, as it was my new beginning. The universe put me in the right place at the right time to meet the people who would support me in realizing what I intended to do in the twilight years.

There will never be enough words to express my gratitude for these gifted women. I will have to settle for thank you and hope they know the depth of these two simple words.

I would also like to acknowledge Laureen Giulian, Author and Founder of Heartfelt Insights, Transformational Journey Facilitator, Quantum Energy Facilitator, Akashic Records & Oracle Card Readings, and The Writer's Patch.

The Writer's Patch is a group of authors who meet every Thursday.

It is where writers feel safe, supported and loved by their fellow authors.

It is in this group that I also met Ashara Gorbert and Antoinette Okai-Koi.

These three beautiful women allowed me to share brief parts of my story with them and reassured me that I had a story to tell that could help others.

After listening to my words, they gave me the book's first line. I had no idea where to begin, and after this vulnerable conversation, I knew exactly what I needed to do.

I have read chapters of the manuscript to them in our Writer's Patch. I always felt nervous about sharing my deepest emotions, but they always responded with love and encouragement—and sometimes tears, too.

I will always be grateful for their non-judgemental support, kindness, and writing knowledge.

I thank my husband, kids, and grandkids for their constant love.

Craig, you deserve a medal for all the encouragement given. I have ideas galore and change my mind daily. You listen and say go for it, no matter how crazy it may sound to your ears.

Leah, you are a mini-me, and I love how we can share our commonalities to get through the fun and challenging days.

Jeffrey, you are my gift after so much loss. We all appreciate your gentleness, thoughtfulness, and patience, especially me.

My grandchildren demonstrate how to be joyful and curious, and I want to be just like them.

All of you give me so much joy and reason to be. THANK YOU.

My mother was my rock after my father died when I was eighteen years old. She was there rain, shine, sleet or snow. She was also there to hold me and just sit with me when my pain was more significant than my desire to carry on. I love you, Mom, and I still miss you every day.

Lastly, it would only be complete if I acknowledged my first husband and our son's father. We went through something together that no marriage expects to survive. We survived, and our last words were our gratitude for each other as parents. We congratulated and acknowledged each other for raising amazing kids who became even better adults.

I am blessed with a rich life of adventure, love, family, and friends.

My husband and I have a saying that we live life every day like we are on vacation.

There is not one person in my life who does not deserve to be part of the acknowledgement.

As we journey through life, many people cross our paths for short periods or as part of our whole lives. They are all essential and intricate parts of getting to where we are.

Each one of you is acknowledged in my heart.

Introduction

One common question posed about the book is, why now?

It has been over 30 years since the event occurred. Why is it important to share your story now?

The answer is so simple if you believe we all have a purpose to act when the time is right, as inspired by the divine. What does the sacred mean to you?

I was enjoying sleeping at the cottage and woke up to a thought that was so powerful and intrusive. It was the idea to write about my infant son's death. It would not let go of me. It was from somewhere outside of myself.

Over the last couple of months, I have been permitting myself to let go of all the things I had been working on that were not serving me anymore. It was time to clear and make room for inspired ideas.

I have asked for help to up my vibrational energies and reveal what I am supposed to do in these twilight years.

I have always known that being an educator was my purpose for my entire career. I loved being a teacher. It fulfilled me. The proverbial water pitcher was always nearby to fill my cup whenever it felt like it was getting depleted. Life always had a way of illuminating all the positives and returning me to a place of gratitude.

It was only late that I found out I had a higher calling.

What stood in my way before to share my story?

I was full of fear.

I had kept this life-changing event in my shadows. I did not talk about it or share my story, even in discussions where women shared their birth stories.

It was something that had become so personal and private.

I did not feel safe sharing and thought somehow it might change things. I was comfortable keeping the most painful event of my life in the shadows. It kept me safe and protected.

It was also over 30 years ago. You did not talk about these things.

Explaining the moments when I received this inspired message is beautiful and spiritual.

It truly is something I have never experienced before. It was outside of me and so powerful. I knew there was no turning back or ignoring this, even though I had free will and could have chosen to go on with my day and brush it off as nonsense.

My journey has led me to incredible opportunities over the last two years.

An accumulation of all my experiences has led me to this one: to share this powerful story of love, forgiveness, and gratitude.

My age and experiences have given me the wisdom to take this story out of the shadows and illuminate it brightly with divine light to help others.

The story that changed me forever within twenty hours, shaped who I was to become, the story that I was too afraid to tell, can illuminate love, forgiveness, gratitude, and peace for other women.

I started to type my story, and the words flowed from my fingers.

I knew I was answering the call of something special.

My words can give comfort to women who are experiencing loss of any kind.

It could be the loss of their life as they knew it before their precious bundle of joy arrived. The realization that no one told them how much everything would change. People try to tell you, but the change is so profound that it is impossible to understand until you experience it.

It could be the loss of their body and the way it was. The fatigue, the swelling breasts now exchanged from sexual parts of ourselves to the food for our child to keep them alive.

It could be the loss of a career path that was the most essential thing in your life before becoming responsible for keeping another human alive.

It could be the loss of the relationship with your husband before the birth of the baby. The once romantic and exciting life has now transformed into diapers and spit.

It could be the lack of sleep and the routines in your life that you once enjoyed.

The loss and grief women feel, even when things are beautiful, and you are grateful for your child, can still feel overwhelming.

I am inspired to author my story to help other women.

I am inspired to author my story to shine the light on my loss and to free myself and my son from the past.

I am so full of love and gratitude as my keys type these words.

I hope to allow my readers to feel loved, supported, cherished, and held in the arms of the divine as they read these words. I am at peace and free.

Chapter One

Contradiction

My milk came on the day of my son's funeral.

I woke up that morning feeling the ache in my uterus. The place where my son had thrived. The cramping and waves of contractions that the miracle of my body was performing to heal itself.

It was also the constant reminder of my empty arms. My excruciating pain of the need to hold my baby and comfort him. The ever-flowing tears that came in tidal waves when I thought of him without me. His mother.

Did he think I had abandoned him? Was he afraid? Was he hungry? Did he need to be changed? Was he warm enough? Did he have any pain?

I understood the ache in my uterus was also contracting due to the hormonal presence of prolactin and oxytocin. My beautiful body knew I was a new mother and was performing all the duties required to nourish my baby and heal my uterus. The presence of these hormones is usually a result of the baby suckling to stimulate the milk to let down.

I would lay in my bed and allow myself to feel my son in my arms. To smell the scent of his newness, to feel his soft skin that had been washed over and kept supple by my amniotic fluid. I could hear his soft moans of pleasure of being held securely and safely. I had never heard them in this presence but experienced his gentle rolling of pleasure and feelings of safety and security inside of my protective womb.

As I dressed for the funeral, I went through the motions without being conscious of my preparations. I only worried if the funeral directors had put on a fresh diaper and dressed him in the onesie I had chosen. Were they keeping him warm in the blanket I had taken to them? The one he was supposed to come home into his lovingly prepared nursery.

I was overwhelmed by the emptiness of my body. The pain was almost unbearable. I didn't know where to turn. Where to sit to find comfort. Where to lay to find rest. The emptiness couldn't even be filled with the delicious food that my mother had prepared for me. I was lost in this world of emptiness.

This complete emptiness, the void, was suddenly filling with tingling in my breasts. I could feel the beginnings of my milk letting down.

The hormones were doing precisely what they were required to do. Was it the presence of my son so near to me in my need to feel him, smell him, touch his soft skin and care for him that was initiating this miracle?

When we arrived at the cemetery for babies, I don't know if we were a little early or if they were running a little late. It doesn't matter. I remember so vividly the tiny white casket being carried by the funeral directors to the grave they had prepared for my son. Seeing the little white casket and the formal funeral directors scurrying across the green lawn surrounded by beautiful big trees was such a contrast.

I could smell the grass and hear the muffled voices of the family and friends who had joined us. I could even hear the giggle of my little daughter, who was only two years old. Her giggle gave me some comfort in the contradictions of this moment. What was happening in my body as a response to my new motherhood was a direct contrast to this tiny white casket and the formal funeral directors.

I could hardly hold my own body weight and had to lean on my husband to stay upright.

While my uterus was cramping and my breasts were becoming fully engorged, I could barely register what was going on around me. Only the tiny white casket that held my son.

The extreme contradictions of the current moment were almost too much to bear.

I do remember feeling the intense emotional pain of those around me. I wasn't the only one experiencing this loss. I felt the love for the child that would never be known in this dimension. I felt his love for his father and me. My mother grieving the loss of her grandchild while watching her own baby in so much pain.

After the funeral, we went back to our home. We asked our family and friends to join us there to share food and be together.

I was still struggling with the pain of engorged breasts, a cramping uterus and the pain of the layers and layers of stitches due to the trauma of my son's delivery.

I knew that this was the first day of the next steps of the process of grief. The most profound grief of grief. A woman's grief. A mother's grief. How would I wake up tomorrow, the next day, and the next day?

I had to believe that God would take care of my little one.

My dad was in heaven, and he would care for him and show him the ropes.

I had to believe there was a greater purpose to this event. Why would a pure little soul who was so loved not be able to survive his birth in a world of medical miracles and the knowledge of our precious doctors?

I knew there had to be a much bigger picture, which would be revealed to me one day. That belief would help me wake up the next morning and the next and the next.

I also had a precious little daughter who needed her mother. I would hold onto that so tightly.

My milk continued to be produced in huge quantities. Over time, I expressed small amounts, and it eventually stopped producing. This is no different from a mother choosing to stop breastfeeding.

I am blessed with a fantastic body that heals itself so efficiently.

I had yet to learn what was ahead.

Love, forgiveness, and gratitude heal all wounds, so I knew there was light.

Chapter Two

SURPRISE

Oooops!

I took the test, and it was positive.

The woman's body is a beautiful vessel of creation. It speaks to us with such clarity and holds the deep wisdom of the universe.

I see the monthly cycle of a woman as a creative dance.

For the first 5 to 10 days of a woman's cycle, it is like a whimsical, flowing dance. The music is light, and the mood is full of energy and freedom. She dances lightly on her bare feet and feels completely aligned in her body, spirit, and mind.

The music feels heavier as she enters the next part of the cycle. Her feet are moving flatter to the floor. The movement is low and more labored, a complete contrast to the vision of the fila of her ovaries gently sending off an egg to move confidently through the fallopian tube. The timing is perfect, and the execution of the movement is intentional and purposeful.

The last part of the cycle is the most magical and has two potential outcomes. Each outcome is as inexplicable as the other.

The miracle of conception and the beginning of a new life or the shedding of the uterine lining to clean and prepare for the next dance. We often think of it as ordinary and an everyday occurrence. It truly is the dance of all dances.

My outcome in this dance was the miracle of conception.

My body had already been whispering to me through different signs: the soreness of my breasts, my love for coffee disappearing, and my feeling more tired than usual.

We had not planned for this pregnancy, as our daughter was still young. She had been colicky, and we were just beginning to enjoy some normal in our lives. We had moved to a new home in a new city, and I had started teaching in a new school board and school.

I was nauseous and felt like an overused dish rag. A little bit put out by this unexpected pregnancy. Our daughter had been colicky beginning at three weeks old. Colicky is an understatement of the level of this poor baby's distress. I took her to the doctor and the chiropractor, and no wise suggestions worked. I put her little car seat, with her in it, on the dryer while it ran. I drove in the car with her with no relief. Babies fall asleep in the car, right? The only thing that seemed to help temporarily was putting her in the bath. It makes sense today as she is a water lover through and through.

At that time, maternity leaves were only four months, so I had been back to teaching, and we were exhausted.

We planned to have a second baby, but it wasn't the best time.

I mention this as these thoughts ravaged my mind for months later in this story.

I was lucky to have a teaching job in a new city. I worked as a special education resource teacher, instructing students individually who needed extra support and guidance. I loved the students but missed the community and chaos of an entire classroom of my own students.

I had heard a new school was being built in our new home's neighborhood, and I decided to apply to teach there. I was conflicted about whether to mention my pregnancy. I still was not showing, so I could get away without saying a thing.

I decided I needed to start this teaching position on the honest right foot, so I told them.

My due date was September, so I would not even be able to start when the school opened its doors for the first time.

It so happened that they appreciated my honesty and believed that family comes first, and I was given the opportunity. I found out later that one of my future colleagues was also expecting and would give birth to her baby in September.

As time passed, I started to feel better, and my energy returned, and we got excited about the new baby coming. At a later ultrasound, we decided to find out what we were having and were thrilled to know we were expecting a little boy. We even picked a name. As far as we were concerned, he was already here. We loved this little life with all our heart.

In June, the school I had been working at graciously threw me a baby shower. It was a surprise on my last day. The staff celebrated me and my baby and gifted us with so much love. They helped me pack my car with all my treasures, and I finished at that school with swollen feet, a big belly, and a happy heart.

I had so much to look forward to.

Summer holidays would be a time to rest and enjoy my family. My daughter would be home with me all summer, and I would spend time at our family cottage with my mom.

Rest and self-care allowed my body's creative dance to flow and ebb. These were the final preparations before September, when I would become a mom again to a sweet baby boy.

Chapter Three

Preparation

The school year had ended, and my thoughtful colleagues had gifted and celebrated me.

It was beautiful to know I had the whole summer to rest and prepare for my baby's arrival in September. I spent much time at the family cottage with my mom and daughter. My family, including my husband, were there on weekends and holidays.

Our first weekend together was Canada Day. It was always the big weekend where we kicked off the next couple of months of sun, fun, water, and family time.

My sister and her two little ones, my daughter, and I stayed with my mom after the weekend festivities were over and everyone returned home.

It was a glorious beginning to the week. The kids were enjoying cousin time, and my mom, sister, and I were catching up on all the conversations we had not had time for during the school year.

Tuesday evening, after dinner, I started to feel some cramping. It was too early for labour, so I just rested on the couch, hoping the Braxton Hicks-type contractions were just my body making room for my growing baby. As the evening went on, they did not go away. In fact, they were intensifying.

Setting the scene of the location of our cottage being water access, which meant a 15-minute boat ride just to get to the marina and then another hour car trip to the nearest hospital, would help explain the possible anxiety which intensified the cramps I was feeling. Possibly, the cramping had not changed, but the anxiety tricked my mind into believing they were more intense.

The fear set in for all of us, and we decided to hit the dark water and get me to the safety of the hospital just in case this was an early labour. We had to wake up our exhausted, sleeping children after a day of fun and frolicking and pack them into the boat.

I was trying so hard to stay calm to allow my body to ease the cramping, but with all the added stress just to get to a hospital, it was proving difficult.

We unpacked the boat and safely transferred everything to one vehicle when we arrived at the marina. We decided to travel together and leave the other car at the marina.

I sat in the passenger seat while my sister drove. My mom, God Bless her, sat in the back with the three kids. My sister's youngest was not even six months old, so he was in his car seat, and my mom was squished between the two little girls.

My little daughter often got car sick, and tonight was no exception. She was crying and saying she was not feeling well. Hearing her cries and not being able to help her was breaking my heart and, of course, increasing the urgency for me to get to the hospital.

My daughter vomited, and we decided to head into Barrie and get a hotel for my sister and the kids. It was halfway to the hospital, but we had to make this easier. We pulled off the highway and got a hotel room. My sister could clean up my daughter, get the little heads back on the pillows, and sleep where they deserved. It would be fun to wake up in a hotel room, too. That was always fun, right?

My Mom and I continued down Highway 400 to the Credit Valley Hospital. We had alerted my husband before we left the cottage, and he would meet us there.

When we arrived in the hospital's parking lot, relief flooded me.

We were admitted quickly to the emergency room, and I was promptly examined by the emergency nurses. After the intake examination, the doctor checked me out more thoroughly. The fetal heart monitor showed that everything was solid and regular. I was not dilated, and my blood work came back stellar.

The doctor told me to rest more and stay in the shade. He saw that my face had enjoyed the sunshine and thought I needed to keep out of the sun. My husband, my mom, and I were so relieved and grateful.

It was, in hindsight, a sign that things were moving along, though.

As we discussed the events and tried to figure out what had caused the cramping, we went back to Saturday, when a friend had come over in her boat to visit. She came into the dock quickly and was going to hit, and I instinctively ran to the end of the dock and gave the boat a big push away with my foot. I could not believe that could have had anything to do with my cramping. I was fit and had stayed active throughout this pregnancy.

Our friend, who had almost hit the dock, was wracked with guilt and felt responsible after our precious son died. It was easy to console her to believe it had nothing to do with the outcome, as I genuinely believed in my heart that this had nothing to do with how things turned out.

My sister and I spent the following weekend unpacking all the gifts I had gotten at my shower and setting up the baby's nursery. We were looking forward to this fun sister bonding experience.

We had so much fun reading the cards and setting everything out to welcome the new baby. It was a magical room where any baby would feel welcomed and loved. We were happy with ourselves, and now I was ready. We could return to the cottage the following week and feel confident that all was right with the world.

My body had other plans.

On Tuesday morning, I had begun to feel those Braxton Hicks cramps again. I had called the doctor at Credit Valley, and they thought it might be a good idea to head down to the hospital. The cramps were coming closer together, and the intensity was not anxiety.

My body is a miraculous vessel of creation.

Being at the cottage and so far from medical attention when you are still a long way away from your due date is generally not concerning, especially when boating and this type of cottaging is the norm.

My unconscious mind was giving me all the information I needed through the magic of my body to get home and stay home. Preparing for the nursery and being closer to the hospital was no accident or coincidence.

It seemed it was time.

We rallied the troops, and my sister and mom came over to get my daughter so they could take care of her. I called my husband, and he came home from work early.

We packed my bag and got into the car.

As we backed out of the driveway, I waved and blew kisses at my supportive, loving family.

We would have a baby and return soon with our son. We were beyond excited to introduce him to all the people who already loved him with all their hearts.

Excitement overrode any apprehension about delivering a baby. It was a regular occurrence—just another day at the office, another mother, another delivery, another baby born.

I was confident in the situation's normalcy and the skills of the obstetricians and nurses I had come to know and trust over the months with my first child and now my second.

We were ready.

Chapter Four
Serenity

The Serenity Prayer:

God grant me,

The Serenity to accept the things I cannot change,

The Courage to change the things I can,

And the Wisdom to know the difference.

In chapter two, I discussed the creative dance of the woman's cycle. The dance can be flowing and light or weighty and stuck. We accept the creative dance in the way it shows up for us. The dance is as unique as the women who share the feminine power.

When we arrived at the hospital, the dance of giving birth was flowing and light.

I had given birth to my daughter at Credit Valley Hospital. It is state-of-the-art, and the care is extraordinary. Her birth occurred in a birthing room tastefully decorated like a living room in a home with an interior designer as the owner. It was comfortable, and there was nothing sterile or hospital-like about it.

I was fortunate to have had a low-risk delivery and was able to have my baby without any drugs or medical interventions. My water had broken at home at about 6:00 a.m., and I was eating pancakes by 9:10. The only person who needed any medical intervention was my husband. He was a person with type one diabetes and had experienced a precipitous low blood sugar just as our daughter was born. He needed attention and was fine after some orange juice and pancakes.

It was the most beautiful sunny wintery day on December 3rd, 1988. The large window in this birthing room shone the sun into the room and was so fitting for the moment of joy we were experiencing.

I was expecting more of the same for my son's birth. We were back at the state-of-the-art hospital, and there was no reason to believe it would be anything but a wonderful experience.

I was settled into a lovely room prepared for women in labour. The nurses set up the fetal monitor, and we waited for the doctor to assess my progress.

The dance so far was soft, and the movement was gentle. I was not experiencing much labour; it was just the odd twinge here and there. I was glad we were at the hospital where our baby was safe and protected by the medical team.

The doctor arrived and began to check my progress. I was only a few centimetres dilated. The baby was in the perfect position, with his head down and engaged in my pelvis—precisely as it was supposed to be. We were in a holding pattern, so we settled in and relaxed.

The dance for other women in the department was a little more furious, and we could hear the cries of the women performing miracles as babies were making their way out into the world.

As time went on, I laboured a little, but I do not remember it being anything but gentle and manageable. I had lots of time to settle in and begin the breathwork I had been taught in the prenatal classes. I remembered how much it helped me with the birth of my daughter, so I believed in breathing and allowed myself to deepen into myself, paying attention to my breathing in and out and in and out.

As an athlete, I was familiar with breathing and aware of the next level efficient breathing could take your body. It was no different here than doing a solo in figure skating: Go to a different place and breathe.

The doctor came back to reassess, and as she felt the outside of my pregnant belly, she noticed a change. Her face showed me that she was not expecting this turn of events. The external palpitations led her to believe that the baby had turned and was now in a breech position.

She called in some reinforcements, and she and the nurses applied pressure to different parts of my abdomen, trying to encourage the baby to move back to the comfy, safe position he had been in before.

My dance began to change quickly.

The pressure they needed to apply on my abdomen was causing me a lot of discomfort, and the dance felt hard. You know that feeling when it seems so much more complicated.

The lightness and breezy feeling are now complex and heavy. I could no longer picture the white flowing gown moving around my body.

The doctor reassured me and said she would do an internal exam and another ultrasound. She wanted to see exactly what position the baby was in, and that was part of her information gathering to help her decide how to proceed now that everything was different.

I trusted the doctors and nurses so much. I worried only about the extra pain that might be ahead of me because of the breech position. I never for a moment worried that my baby was in any compromising place. Only two weeks before the long weekend in July at the cottage, I had been to the obstetrician, and his exact words were, "Beautiful pregnancy, fit mom, risk-free." I believed him, and at that time, it was precisely the right words for the situation.

After the ultrasound and the internal exam, the doctor came to discuss her plan with us.

She had decided that she was going to break my water and lower the baby's behind into the birth canal with her hand. She thought that would get things started and that her support for him would allow her to safely position him exactly where she wanted him to be.

She warned me that once my water was broken, the labour would move quickly. She also decided it was wise to give me an epidural. That would support me with the intense pain of breech labour and help my muscles relax so my baby could move through without any resistance.

When she said she was going to deliver him vaginally, I wondered in the back of my mind why she wouldn't just schedule a c-section. I pushed off the thoughts as we so often do.

Those messages come from our unconscious mind that we so frequently ignore. I didn't even ask about it.

My husband was more in tune with the situation, and he felt a c-section was a safer situation, but the doctor was confident she had it, and all would be just as it was supposed to be.

I struggle with the details of the next part.

My husband passed away five years ago, so I cannot ask him. He was the only one other than the doctor who could give me the information I was foggy about.

I do believe the next step was the epidural.

My husband, with diabetes, took a needle at least three times a day and did not like seeing anyone else get needles. He opted to wait outside while the anaesthesiologist got me all hooked up. After a few minutes, he mustered up the courage and wanted to be there with me for the procedure. They had already started; it was a sterile environment, and the doctor said he would have to wait.

I appreciated his change of heart.

If I recall correctly, the following steps were when the doctor broke my water.

I will never forget this part. As the doctor lowered his little behind into my birth canal, she looked up at us and asked if we knew what we were having. We said yes, we did, a little boy.

She had not wanted to spoil the surprise, but she could feel his little testicles in her hand.

It was a moment of pure joy as this little bundle was right there in her hand, and it would be only a short time before I got to hold him in my arms and whisper his name into his ear. I could touch his baby skin, softly kiss his forehead, count his fingers and toes and promise to love him unconditionally for the rest of my life.

The contractions were still relatively mild, but I did have an epidural, so I most likely wasn't even aware of them in my physical body. I could see the fetal monitor beside my bed, and my heart rate would go up and down, which indicated I was having a contraction.

We did this for a while; it's just us waiting.

A nurse came in to check, and she watched the monitor.

Suddenly, she was working quickly to lower the head of my bed and put an oxygen mask over my face. I could tell by the look on her face this wasn't a routine maneuver. I felt frightened for the first time, completely out of control and at the mercy of the medical team.

Eventually, whatever had happened must have righted as I was sitting up again, and the oxygen was taken away. Telling this piece of the birth story is relevant, and I will explain just how much of a window into the future it was later.

I was now fully dilated and ready to deliver my breech baby vaginally.

I did not feel the contractions, so whenever it was time to push, the doctors and nurses would let me know, and I would do my part.

There are so many things that come to your mind after.

I had a terrible headache.

I had watched a movie the night before about a woman who was having a baby. She had been experiencing a bad headache all day. When she was delivering her baby and pushing, she had an aneurysm, and she died.

I remember feeling afraid that my headache was not just the dance of hormonal fluctuations which I had experienced my whole female life throughout my cycles. I allowed myself to feel fear that if I pushed too hard, I would have an aneurysm.

It sounds so ridiculous now as I write it, but at the time, it was real. This fear during my own son's delivery also became part of the grief story profoundly.

Everything seemed going as it was supposed to be, but then it wasn't.

The baby's heart was decelerating with every push. I know this is a normal part of the last part of the delivery, with a return to regular heart rate after the push is over.

My baby's heart was decelerating, and it was not going back up. I could see the concern again on the obstetrician's face and the exchanges between her and the obstetrical nurses.

My husband was videotaping.

The doctor told him to stop the camera.

I heard the doctor tell the nurses to call the pediatrician on call STAT.

From my love of medical drama shows, I knew what STAT meant. We needed a baby doctor and were in a hurry. She also requested forceps.

I again felt the excruciating pain of them pushing on my abdomen, even through the epidural. I could see her discard the forceps and saw both of her arms up to her elbows inside of my body.

We knew this was not a good situation, and I finally wondered why I was not having an emergency C-section.

It was too late.

My baby's head was stuck. My cervix had locked over his head, and the doctor needed to get him out immediately. I didn't know this, but his heartbeat had gone so low it was almost nonexistent.

She was finally able to get him out. The room was filled with people waiting for him.

They took him right away to what looked like an emergency room trauma space.

The nurse stood at my head. I asked her if our baby was okay. She said she just didn't know yet. They are doing everything they can for him right now. We could see them bent over him, using every available skill.

My husband put his face over mine, and we prayed. We prayed, and we prayed together.

I said to him, "Do we pray for him to live or to go to heaven?"

I knew he had experienced a lot of trauma in this delivery. I knew that there must have been a lot of oxygen deprivation for my darling little boy as he tried so hard to make his way out to his awaiting parents.

We prayed and prayed and surrendered to God for his will to be done—for the best for our little boy. We then prayed for ourselves and surrendered ourselves to God.

Chapter Five

The Reality

Our prayers were interrupted by the doctor approaching us from the side of the room where they were working on our son.

I saw the doctor and noticed the nurse at the side of my head on my right shuffle around the bed and move over to the left. The doctor came up on the right side.

I have such vivid memories of details.

I looked at the doctor. Our eyes locked, and I managed to choke out the words I needed to ask. "Is our baby boy okay?"

She continued to look right into my eyes and answered, "We did everything we could, but he did not make it."

I am a quieter crier. I am almost embarrassed in moments of sadness that bring tears.

At this moment, I screamed the word "no," which came from the depths of my soul. I shook, screamed, and cried all at the same time, with the word "no" being the only word I could capture to express my gut-wrenching pain.

"No, No, No…"

I am a runner. I choose flight over fight in times of intense stress.

I was trapped in my body.

My legs wouldn't work because of the epidural.

My body had also been traumatized by the delivery. Ripped apart as the doctor tried desperately to free my son's head from my own cervix that had clamped down on his head and tiny shoulder.

I wanted to run and feel free of this misery.

If I could run, I could breathe copious amounts of oxygen into my lungs and then breathe the oxygen out, reminding me of the strength of my body. This feeling had always been a go-to for me.

Freeing my mind from the thoughts that were too much to handle.

Feel my strong legs pushing me forward faster and faster. My hair in the wind, and my feet hitting the ground. Run until I could not run anymore. Exhausted, tired, and clearer.

I could not run. I was trapped in this room, in my body, with this excruciating pain.

The doctor needed to repair my wounded physical body. It took a long time as she needed to stitch the layers of ruptured tissue before she could stitch the last of the wound on the outside.

The words I just wrote have resonated with me in a way that I never have put together before. The wounds on the inside had to be repaired before she could stitch the wounds on the outside.

I had no idea what lay ahead to heal the wounds inside my soul before I could heal the outside. I am writing this thirty-four years later and telling my story now in hopes of my final healing and releasing my son to his freedom.

After the repair work was completed and I continued to weep tears that I felt would never stop, they asked me if I wanted to hold my baby.

My arms were aching to hold him. I needed to comfort him. My conscious mind had not caught up with the reality. My body contradicted reality. I had just given birth, and that meant I had a baby to care for who needed me.

The nurse brought him to us.

He was wrapped in a blue baby blanket, and he was cleaned up in the way a new baby is cleaned. He was exactly as if he was alive, breathing, crying, and hungry for his first colostrum. The smell of a new baby filled my nostrils.

His tiny body was warm, and he looked so peaceful.

We counted his toes and his fingers and kissed his sweet face. I noticed he had marks on his forehead where the doctor had frantically tried the forceps.

We commented on how much he was a Johnson. He had the handsome square jaw of his dad and his uncles.

My husband wanted to hold him, so I gently placed him in his arms.

He turned his back to me. I could not hear his quiet crying, but I could see his shoulders moving up and down as he was wracked with the sobs of a broken heart. To witness the depth of his pain in his physical body's movements shook me.

We had both lost our infant child. Our dreams for his future. Our excitement to introduce him to our daughter and the rest of our family. His first tooth, his first step, the first time he would sleep through the night, the first solid meal, his first Christmas, his first love. We would bear the pain of this loss of his firsts in the months to come.

At that moment, I could only say and feel "NO."

I was sitting with my baby in my arms, knowing the time to hold him and love him in this physical form was coming close to being over.

The door opened to the room, and our long-time friend and sister-in-law walked in.

Our reality was about to be solidified in a powerfully contradictory way.

She came in all bubbly and excited. Full of joy when we welcome a new life into this world. Love for us and this new baby she could introduce to her son as his new cousin.

She approached the bed and asked if she could hold the new bundle.

The reality came crashing in as I realized she did not know. How could this have happened? I still cannot imagine it to this day, but it was happening.

The words tumbled out of my mouth. No gentle approach to sharing this news. Just grief spoke the words of my reality. I blurted out, "The baby died."

It was like someone had physically pushed her back away from me and the baby. She kept stepping back until she was leaning on the wall. Her body had deflated, and she just stared. I do not remember whether there were any words. I remember her standing against the wall, looking at us for the longest time. Sometimes, there are no words.

She stayed against the wall for a while. I do not remember when she left or said goodbye.

The doctor came in to ask how we were doing and if we needed anything. I find this hard to believe, but now I think we default to our true selves even in times of trauma.

I was someone who cared about others even in my worst situations.

I asked her how she was doing.

As a doctor and mother, I remarked that this must be hard for her. I knew she was a mother of four children, so putting herself in my shoes was not a stretch. She said her biggest concern was us and our loss. She mentioned that it was so kind of me to think of her when my grief was so raw and honest at that moment.

She asked us if we would like to keep a bit of his hair, and they wanted to take a picture of him for us. They needed to take him away from me, but they promised they would bring him right back.

After he came back, we held him for a little longer. I noticed his tiny body was beginning to feel cold. The nurse said we only had a few more minutes and would have to say goodbye.

She came into the room to take him. Through my wrenching sobs, I asked if they would leave his blanket on him. Please do not take his blanket off. He likes it wrapped tightly.

My reality was I would never hold my baby in the physical sense again. I would not keep him warm on my chest wrapped in his blanket, which I had decided, as his mother, he liked wrapped tightly.

Only a few hours ago, I was awaiting the birth of our second child. Such anticipation and excitement. Now, we were saying goodbye to him forever in this realm of the physical world. The contradiction was too much to bear. As I write these words thirty-four years later, I wonder how we survived these moments. It was like my heart was being torn into shreds.

The emptiness was truly setting in.

They came to tell us I was being moved to the medical floor. They did not want me on the maternity floor where babies were being born and families were welcoming the new ones to the world. I appreciated that gesture.

As we settled into our new room on the medical floor, the reality kept coming.

I was so exhausted, and it was now the middle of the night. My husband sat in a chair beside the bed, and we just stared. No words came, just the emptiness.

I kept dozing off because I was so tired. For a moment of sleep, I was freed from this reality. My conscious mind turned off in sleep. I would wake, and reality would hit me like a ton of bricks, and the tears would flow. I remember it feeling like a jolt of electricity, and my body would physically jerk as I awakened to the darkness and emptiness—the reality.

Tears and the only word I could utter, "No," were all I could muster up until sleep retook me for a moment of peace.

We got through the night, and my mom wanted to bring my daughter to see us. It would be good as we waited for the doctor to check my physical body.

I will never forget the feeling I had when my bouncy little daughter came into the room. I felt aloof and lost. I did not know how to feel that instinctual mothering that I had always felt with this precious gift. She climbed onto my lap on the hospital bed and was so pleased to see me. I hugged her and loved her deeply, yet I felt so withdrawn and unsure.

As time went on, my mothering instincts came back full on, and she became my reason to be. She became my reason to wake up, dress, make food, care for our home, and live. She gave me a reason to have faith, love, forgive, and carry on.

Finally, the doctor came later that morning.

She wanted me to stay in the hospital another day and night for observation. I thanked her for her concern and asked for my release papers as soon as possible. I needed to get out of that place.

I needed a shower so badly. My husband held onto me and walked me to the shower room.

I love water.

Along with running and pushing my body to the edge, water is my other go-to in intense stress.

I let the water pour over me and wash all the night before off my body and into the drain. I was still so sore. The water felt good on my hurting female body parts. I honored my body as the water flowed. It was not my body's fault. It was not my fault.

Blame was not what I was seeking at that moment.

Cleansing my body and feeling the water flow from my head, over my body, and off my feet into the drain was a way of cleansing the physical events of the night before.

When we returned to my room, I dressed in the clothes I had prepared to wear home as the mother to a new son.

We left the hospital and went home to begin to plan our next goodbye for our baby.

I needed to be with my family at home. The safe place where love surrounded us. We could begin to grieve in the privacy of our own space with the people who meant so much to us.

I realized after my daughter had her children the grief my own mother was experiencing. To witness the pain that you have no power to stop in your own child while grieving the loss of your grandchild is most certainly a space no one wants to find themselves. I fully appreciate the grace and strength of my mother. I hope she knows how much she meant to both of us and that I could not imagine having done this part of my life without her.

The dance of my current reality ebbed and flowed as the emotions gripped me.

The movement between remembering the idea of the miracle of childbirth and the realization that it is a gift. It is not without danger and unexpected outcomes.

My body was a vessel of creation.

My child was "born an angel."

He existed. He was loved, and he loved. His name was chosen to honor his grandfathers, and he had a bright future full of potential.

I began to realize my biggest fear was that he would be forgotten. He did not have a chance to imprint his mark on this world. I have no idea the exact science of how this fear manifested the way I grieved for my son. I do believe it played a significant part.

The death of my son was a contradiction to the way I lived my life.

My faith and my core values would be challenged, and the woman who walked into Credit Valley Hospital on July 10th, 1990, to give birth to a baby boy would not exist again.

My fear that my son would be forgotten was compounded by the loss of myself and the person I had once been.

One day, we are who we are. Within hours, a single event forever changes us.

We have a choice.

Even in the darkness and the emptiness, we have the power to choose.

Chapter Six
Back to Normal
Nothing is Normal

We left the hospital and returned to our home in Cambridge, Ontario.

When I walked in the door, my daughter and Mother were there to greet us. We lived in a beautiful home that was always clean, fresh, and well cared for. My mom ensured we arrived home with a bathed, dressed daughter and a clean house.

Interestingly, simple things can comfort us when we experience difficult situations. My mom knew exactly what I would need when I walked into the house.

On the first day or two, I spent a lot of time in bed. It was hard to get up and face life.

I did not want to see anyone or talk to anyone. My mom and husband were careful to screen visitors on my behalf.

There was one visitor my mom thought I would like to see.

As I made my way down our stairs, I saw one of the teachers from my school with a huge basket of fruit, chocolate, and so many more beautiful things. She was kind and caring, letting me know everyone had me in their prayers. It meant a lot to me and my family.

I had another visitor during the first couple of days at home.

My sister had given birth to my nephew, who was only a couple of months old and a little boy. She was unsure about bringing him to see me, but we decided it would be the best medicine.

One of the most challenging things I did was to take this baby into my arms and hold him so close to me. The tears flowed, and my heart broke all over again. After having him for a few minutes, his warm little body and his sounds were the best medicine. I loved my nephew more than life, and between him, my niece, and my sweet daughter, the little people in my life kept me going.

This little nephew of mine was also very colicky. We would giggle that he cried so hard and often to make me feel better. I could hold him and love him and then go home and sleep.

We were fortunate enough to have a pool in our yard. On the second night home, it was a gorgeous, warm July evening.

We had been sitting out in the yard, and I had my daughter lying on my lap. Snuggling felt so good. As we prepared to go in and put her to bed, I decided to dive into the pool for a quick swim. Our pool was deep, and I could dive deeply into the soothing water. As I dove and swam deeply down to the bottom, I felt a chill in my body that I had never experienced before. It was a deep bone chill that swept throughout every cell. I have no idea what it was about, but it was the contradiction of the warm evening in July and what my body, soul, and mind had just gone through.

As days and weeks went on, there were things I remember as being so comforting.

The principal at my new school, whom I had only met a couple of times, was one of those people that you know you are in the presence of such goodness when he is around you. He had been a former priest who had left the priesthood to follow his heart, marry, and have a family. He now was the proud father of eight children.

He would stop by every Tuesday for the whole summer to visit. He would listen and offer counsel if it felt right.

I remember talking about being afraid to try again for another baby. His wise words told me that you have two choices: You can be a plastic rose and protect yourself from being broken, or you can choose to be a natural rose that is delicate and vulnerable. His powerful words gave me the courage to consider being fragile and vulnerable again.

We did have a couple of visits back to the cottage. It was a place of peace and tranquility, and we have so many memories of happiness and joy there.

Every summer, there was a regatta that was fun for both adults and kids. On the Sunday evening of the regatta, there was always a party for the adults. It was a big campfire, and we had a covered dance floor that we danced the night away at this yearly party.

My husband and I decided it would be good for us to go. All our friends would be there. People who were safe and who loved us. It was only about three weeks after our son's death, but some fun seemed like a good idea.

I saw a friend there who had dedicated his life to being a surgeon. He looked after me when I was twenty-seven years old when I had a severe back injury. I briefly talked to him, but I kept feeling his eyes on me as the evening went on. I would see him looking at me through the crowd. His face was full of pain, and I knew, as a surgeon, he felt a collective consciousness as part of the medical oath to not harm and the tragedy of this event that never should have taken place. It was almost as if he could see into my soul and feel my pain.

Without spoken words, his acknowledgment would come to mean even more as time passed. I discovered that people did not know what to say or how to act, so they often would just pretend it did not happen.

Later, at the party in Regatta Cottage Flavor, my sister and I had to hit the trees for a pee.

We giggled as we often did when hanging out together, laughing until we cried in the bush with our pants down. I was released from everything for a few moments and felt happy. Even though it was only a glimpse for a few moments, it was happiness.

We often feel guilty when we feel happy for the first time after losing someone we loved so much. I have heard, and I believe, that our loved one is letting us go, if only for a moment. It is the hope of our loved ones that we will heal and live our lives.

One step at a time, one moment at a time.

My husband and I walked along the beach that night at the party and talked about having another baby. We felt overwhelmed by the thought of starting all over again with another pregnancy and getting through the fear of another delivery. We both concurred that we wanted another child, and we would be that natural rose. We might bend and even break, but we needed to try again.

We had a doctor's appointment scheduled in a couple of weeks, and we would discuss these thoughts about our plans with her.

It is odd how people respond to these situations.

People thought we needed to see a lawyer and sue the doctor for malpractice.

We decided that we needed to at least chat with a lawyer, and a good friend set us up with a lawyer who fought on behalf of doctors who were sued by patients. I know that sounds crazy, but we did not want to be told we had a good case and be set up for years of more hurt. We decided to talk to this person who could honestly tell us where we were at.

During the appointment, it became clear, as his voice began to sound muffled, I could not listen to any more lawyers say we could win a case. It would not matter whether we could win a case and get a lot of money. It would not bring back our son. He was gone. We had to deal with that reality and do our best to heal our hearts. We thanked the lawyer and appreciated the time he had given us at no cost. His advice was truthful and in our favor, but we knew it was not the road for us to take.

I believed that the hospital would investigate the death of my child due to decisions that were made during his birth and make sure that things would be put into place to ensure it did not happen again to a trusting couple.

Medical errors happen. I wish this had not happened to us, but there is always a reason, and sometimes we must accept the outcomes.

The title of this chapter is back to normal but not normal.

My mom and I used to go to the mall with my daughter in the early weeks after the death of my son. We would walk around, go to the food court, and try to enjoy the time together.

One day, we were sitting in the food court, and people were nearby laughing and enjoying themselves immensely. I guess I was entering the next part of the journey with grief as I wanted to yell out to them. I wanted to scream my baby just died. How can you be so happy? It is not fair. That question again, I had asked myself so many times in the last few weeks. WHY?

I know it is the craziest thing, but the emotions of grief can come in so many weird ways.

I shared what I was thinking now with my mom, and it felt better to say it out loud. Talking about it confirmed the ridiculousness of the anger being taken out on happy people.

The anger and guilt would rear its ugly head many more times on this journey. The bargaining and then back to the disbelief.

For that moment in time, it passed, and we went on with our mall walking. Finding a little bit of peace and happiness.

Chapter Seven
The Roller Coaster Ride That Is Grief

"Grief is the price we pay for love."

– Queen Elizabeth II

The summer ended, and it was time to go back to work.

I had decided to return even though I was entitled to my maternity leave.

I loved teaching and was embarking on a new journey, opening a new school up the road from where we lived.

I did not see the value in staying home. Staying busy was more authentic to my grief experience.

We discovered we could start trying for another baby after six months. Since it was only September, I would carry on.

There were a few situations that came up that revealed to me that even though I was carrying on, I was still grieving deeply.

I was invited to a girls' weekend at a cottage in Muskoka. I decided to go as I felt it would be good to get away and spend time with ladies.

One of the women had just had a baby, too.

She, like me, was carrying a little extra baby weight and was still working at getting her body back to the level of health and wellness that felt good.

I quickly learned that it was going to be a tough weekend.

I know the women were not trying to hurt me. I knew that it was the lack of awareness and understanding on their part of what to say and what to do. They spoke to the other woman about her delivery and acknowledged that she had just had a baby, and I stood by feeling sick to my stomach.

I did not want to take away from her experience and joy; I just could not believe there was no word or question about how I might feel. I could not wait for the weekend to be over. I spent a lot of the rest of the time just trying to get through the conversations and not be the person who ruined the fun for everyone else.

I did not want people to feel afraid to talk to me about it or bear witness to the little boy ready to enter the world and knock it out of the park.

Forgiveness and love were the only things I could do. The women were not to blame. Thirty-four years ago, it was uncomfortable; ignoring it was the easiest way to cope. I felt the height of the grief again as it peaked after the weekend. I was triggered so profoundly, and it took a while to get back on my feet. My worst fear was that the whole situation and the little boy I loved would be forgotten had played out in real-time at the cottage.

The school was where I could transport myself to a different reality. I had a great class of Grade 7's, and it was busy getting the new school's policies and procedures all established. It felt good.

Being a Catholic school, the priest would come, and we, the staff and the students, would go into the gym, sit on the plastic chairs, and have mass.

I am not Catholic, but I loved the Catholic mass, especially for the music.

I was sitting there on my plastic chair, and one of my favourite hymns was being played. I was unprepared, and the emotions I had held at bay flooded my throat, and I could not hold them back. I had to leave, and I went to the bathroom and sobbed and sobbed. Two of the staff came into the washroom to check on me. They wondered if maybe I was staying too busy and was not allowing myself to go through the grief. They were right.

There were a couple of other things that jolted me out of denial.

Guilt that I did not push hard enough because of my headache. It had been my fault.

Anger that my husband did not push harder for a cesarian section.

Guilt that I had not pushed harder for a cesarian section.

I was angry that my husband seemed to be doing better than I was. Why did he not care as much as I did?

Bargaining and unrealistic thoughts.

My husband was one of those men who could fix anything.

One day, I believed he would come home with the car seat in the back of our van and have our baby in it. He would fix this.

Anger and fighting between us became nasty and unmanageable. We said things to each other that could not be taken back. They were not what either of us believed. It was the pain of talking and the need to blame someone.

We finally decided it was time to get some help. It was not easy to come by, but I found a support group for grieving parents. We decided there was nothing to lose, and we were not in a good place.

The group was a lifesaver. Hearing other parents tell their stories and providing credibility to the fact that we were not crazy and were just like others experiencing this grief was a gift to both of us.

We also learned that seventy-five percent of marriages do not survive this loss. Each parent is grieving the same loss. It is a roller coaster ride. One person in the marriage cannot pull the other off the roller coaster to safety and solid footing because they are on the same roller coaster.

The loss and the grief are so profound for both that neither can step up and be the rock for the other.

We only went a few times, as it was enough to set us back on a more loving, kind, forgiving, and grateful path.

Before the decision to seek out help, the grief almost buried us.

We were not going to let it bury us.

We had our daughter who needed us.

We had decided we wanted to try again for another baby.

Despite our wounded hearts, we had much to be grateful for and look forward to.

I did not know any other way but to just keep fighting.

Chapter Eight
Ain't No Mountain High Enough

"Cause baby, there ain't no mountain high enough,

Ain't no valley low enough,

Ain't no river wide enough,

To keep me from getting to you, babe."

This is one of my favourite songs.

I love the beat and the rhythm. The uplifting lilt to this song.

It also was always a song of inspiration and strength for me.

If I ran with a big hill ahead, I would quickly find this track and turn it up. Singing the lyrics at the top of my lungs while I ran always motivated me and pushed me up that hill.

The original songwriters, Nick Ashford and Valerie Simpson, were newcomers to the music scene and submitted the song to Motown in late 1966. The song was inspired by Nick Ashford's looking up at the skyscrapers in Manhattan and realizing they were the mountains that were not high enough to keep him from his dreams.

No mountain was high enough to keep me from having another baby.

As part of my prenatal care, I joined a moderate fitness class. It was held in the gym at the new school just up the street, which was perfect. It gave me a sense of community and a place to work out.

This new baby, who we found out was a boy, also had ideas about when he would arrive in the world.

He decided seven weeks before his due date that he wanted to get out.

The doctors, of course, had other ideas. I was put on bed rest in the hospital for two weeks. The first week, I could not get out of bed to go to the bathroom. Fun times.

When he was still inside six weeks before his due date, they allowed me to use the washroom and go for short walks on the floor. I was bored to tears. I missed my students, my daughter, and my husband, but it was what I needed to do to protect this little prize.

The doctors and nurses would come in, stick their heads in the door, and remark that I was still there. I learned after the baby was born that no one wanted to be on shift when I decided to go into labor.

Five weeks before the due date, the doctor said I could go home and run if I wanted. The baby was ready.

This baby decided he was on his way four weeks before the scheduled delivery. It was fast and furious, like my daughter. My husband had to drive over the curb to get around a bus to get me to the hospital. We had decided to stay in Cambridge this time, so it was a short drive.

I had the baby in a birthing chair, and I did not have any drugs or even an episiotomy. I got to watch the baby in a mirror, and it was beautiful.

He came out screaming, and he was a tiny little guy. The pediatrician came to check on him and said he was little but strong and healthy.

This time, my mom and other family members could come and see him, hold him, and wrap themselves in our joy. It was precisely the way it was supposed to be.

Even though it was exactly as it was supposed to be, the demons kept trying to invade my confidence and trust.

I kept waking up in the night and asking the nurses if I could look at him in the nursery. I was afraid to believe he was okay and we were okay.

I know my fears were irrational, but I could not shake the idea that I could not lose this precious bundle of second chances.

I had climbed that mountain, and even though there were times when I would get to a plateau and think I could not go any further, the dream of this baby was so inspired. He was never to replace the child we lost. He was his little personality waiting to shine.

Our other child was born an angel and would always be our angel.

The woman I worked with at the school told me that after all was good, the baby was home, and I was healthy that I was so aloof through this pregnancy.

I was unaware of it, but I believe she was right.

Our minds are so strong.

Our unconscious mind protects us twenty-four-seven. It only gives us what we can handle. My extraordinary mind gave me what I needed to get through, what I needed to grow this baby and get him out safe and sound.

A gift from the divine at the right time. It is all part of a bigger picture that we must trust and surrender to. I believe that with all my heart.

"If you need me, call me, no matter where you are,

No matter how far, don't worry, baby,

Just call my name; I'll be there in a hurry,

You don't have to worry."

I surrendered, and I climbed the mountain. The gift at the top of that mountain was worth every gruelling step.

Chapter Nine
THE COLLECTIVE CONSCIOUSNESS

I am so fortunate to be a grandmother to two amazing little boys.

The first grandson was born with no birth complications. He was a big boy, and my daughter pushed him out with no epidural and like a true champion.

I got to be the birth coach along with her husband; it was the experience of a lifetime.

My daughter had chosen a midwife for her delivery; it was her husband and my job to act as the stirrups. She would push against us, and we would talk her through each contraction. It was such a gift to have that opportunity and to be there to bear witness to the birth of this beautiful little boy.

The pregnancy of her second son was much more challenging. She had a great deal of back pain, and she was so fatigued. Of course, you do not get to rest when you have a young one to look after. Her fatigue seemed to be more than just the extra load.

As time went on and her due date was approaching, she was experiencing a lot of severe cramps that seemed to be more than Braxton hicks.

The midwife who was looking after this delivery kept suggesting that she just stay home until the contractions were closer together. I was alarmed at this because my daughter was experiencing such harsh cramps. It sure seemed to me that she was in labor.

Finally, after not getting the go-ahead from the midwife to come to the hospital, we decided to go anyway. We were frightened at home, and things seemed to progress despite the time between the contractions not getting any closer together.

When we arrived at the hospital, my daughter was in so much pain it was tough to witness. The nurses were wonderful and got her ready and settled into the labor room. They got the fetal monitor on the baby and were watching closely all that was happening.

The midwife finally came and felt that everything was as it was supposed to be.

Time was marching on, and my intuition was screaming something was wrong. I was trying not to be dramatic and go to an unnecessary place. The baby was just not progressing into the birth canal, and his mother was in excruciating pain.

The midwife ordered an epidural, and the anesthesiologist came to get her all set up.

She was able to relax into the delivery with the epidural cutting some of the pain, which caused her to tense and stress, making everything more difficult for the baby.

I looked at the monitors and noticed that the baby's heart rate was decelerating as it was supposed to during contractions. The problem was not recouping and returning to the expected heart rate.

The nurses came in and had my daughter get up on all fours on the bed, and they tried to maneuver the baby. They were trying to reposition him as I believe they were concerned about his body compressing on the umbilical cord.

Things could have been better.

I started to get frantic, but I did not want my daughter to see my distress. I left the room and called my sister. She heard the panic in my voice and realized I was going to a dark place in my history. She advised me to return to the room and advocate for my grandbaby and daughter. I would do whatever I had to do to get action.

The midwife was a big disappointment. She stood back and did not respond to this situation at all. I saw the nurse with us the whole time, trying to talk to her. She was forcibly pointing out that the heart rate was going down to fifty and not coming back up.

The nurse left the room for a minute.

When she was gone, I went to the nurse's station and said something was wrong with this delivery, and we needed help.

When I returned to the room, I went to the nurse to speak to her about my concerns. She looked at me with knowing eyes and let me know the obstetrician had been called and was on her way. She had gone over the midwife's head and done what needed to be done.

I left the room to gather myself, as I was not holding it together. I saw the doctor get off the elevator, hopping down the hallway and taking her boots off as she ran.

The next thing we knew, there were many people in the room. Some were assisting, others were taking careful notes, and a pediatric doctor was there, ready to support the baby when he arrived.

The obstetrician took charge and reassured us that the little boy causing all this worry would be out in no time. The head nurse approached me, ushered me to the doctor's side, and told me to watch my grandbaby come into this world. I was shaken to the core but wanted to see this miracle happen.

When my grandson made his appearance, he was rushed to an awaiting trauma area that they had wheeled in along with the expert pediatrician. They massaged his chest and gave him oxygen, and we held our breath with anticipation.

In a moment, they decided to take him from the room.

The head nurse explained that they did not want him to code in front of us or have us witness the protocols they would have to administer if this did happen.

My daughter watched them take him out of the room, grabbed my hands, and spoke the words I will never forget: "We are in trouble, aren't we, Mom?"

I responded with an honest answer. I did not know. That was the truth.

I aged about twenty years while we waited, held hands, and cried.

I kept asking myself how this could happen again. It cannot happen again.

I went out into the hallway to see if I could find anything out, and I saw the doctor walking towards the room with our little baby. He was as good as rain.

The relief that flooded every cell of my body gave me cold shivers and made my knees buckle.

To watch my daughter and her husband receive their little bundle, which was alive, pink, and healthy, was the greatest gift I could ever imagine.

I called this chapter collective consciousness because everyone in the room worked together on a level greater than anything that happens when there is ego. We collectively related on a level that was connected to saving that baby.

I believe the midwife was all about ego. Her ego and lack of action almost put our family into a place of unbelievable loss and trauma.

We spoke to the nurse after a week or so, and she was open and honest about how close we came. She also did not hide that the situation did not have to be how it played out and held the midwife responsible. We never knew what happened to the midwife. All I can hope for is that her practice changed dramatically so that nothing like our situation could ever happen again to another family awaiting their gift from God.

I was retraumatized again after that experience, and it took me a long time to get peace.

Two weeks after my grandson was born, COVID-19 hit, and we were unable to see him other than through a glass window. It was challenging, but I knew along with my son, he was my second chance baby.

I believe with all my heart that the collective consciousness of those of us in the room and the divine and kindred spirits of my son, mom, and dad were there to change this outcome.

We will never take for granted the lives of those boys.

We are enriched daily by their joyful presence and how they grasp life with that gorgeous child innocence. Fantasy is their world, and playing in it with them is a welcome relief from the worries and realities of today.

We are blessed beyond blessed.

When we come together with a common goal to make the world a safer, better place for all of us, and there is only that greater good within our scope and no ego attached, we can save babies' live.

Chapter Ten
Love, Forgiveness, Gratitude, Abundance

It is May 2024, and I just turned 67 years old as I write my story to share and inspire other women to find the courage to love yourself enough, forgive yourself enough, and find gratefulness in everyday activities. To discover and be aware of all the abundance that surrounds you.

At 67 years of age, I am a retired school teacher, a mother of two exceptional adult children, the mother-in-law of two fantastic adult partners in life to my kids, a grandmother of two sweet boys, and a happy wife. I also have a cute little white cockapoo dog who fills my life with laughter and unconditional love.

I have a life that is filled with abundance of all kinds. The most precious of this abundance is love, forgiveness, and gratitude.

The man I speak of in my story was my first husband. He passed away in 2018.

We were given many mountains to climb over our married life.

We separated in 2007.

Even though we were separated, we continued to live as a family, celebrating holidays and special events together. Our children and grandchildren were our most precious gifts, and choosing love and positivity and always remembering why we married in the first place kept our family peaceful and enduring.

I am so grateful for that choice, as who knew we would lose him so young.

Our grandson was only a baby, and our kids were only beginning the journey of marriage and parenting. We had so much to share and enjoy as parents and grandparents.

Our last words to each other were to celebrate the wonderful kids we had raised together. We were so proud, and we let each other know it was a team effort and that we could not have done this fantastic job without each other's support.

What a gift this conversation was when, a few days later, he passed away from a sudden heart attack.

It was another heart-breaking journey of resilience and courage.

Our family was strong and united, and we confronted the loss of a dear father and my co-parent and co-grandparenting partner with a commitment of love and gratitude.

Knowing he would meet our son on the other side was a sense of comfort.

He could finally be with his baby boy, who would now have been twenty-eight years old in earthly years. I knew my parents had been there with him for many years already. There was one more family member to join him so he could show them the ropes of the other world.

I married my second husband in October 2020.

We had dated when we were in high school.

I believe in the blueprint for our lives long before we arrive. Having faith that everything is the way it is supposed to be at the right time can be difficult, especially when we feel pain and suffering along the way.

My current husband and our lives intertwined briefly over forty-nine years ago.

He came into my life two weeks after my father passed away when I was eighteen years old. I later realized that his purpose was to make me laugh and distract me with fun activities, and he loved me. He got me through another difficult time in my life.

Our lives needed to go in a different direction, even though I was heartbroken and did not understand the feelings of more loss and grief.

His wife of thirty-three years passed away from ALS in 2015.

After all these years, we have reunited and created a life together.

Since I retired from teaching, I have dabbled in different passions to keep me involved and a part of the community.

My curiosity about the spiritual, faithful, energetic side of life became something I found interesting and well worth looking at in more depth.

I have learned so much and feel transformed in so many ways.

I have found true peace and freedom. I believe in the present moment and love life as it is.

I found the practice of Ho'oponopono.

Self-directed ho'oponopono is a practice and technique based on the Hawaiian philosophy of reconciliation and forgiveness. It involves taking personal responsibility for one's own healing by clearing negative emotions, thoughts, and memories.

The four critical phrases used are: "I love you. I am sorry. Please forgive me. Thank you."

By repeating these phrases, individuals aim to release internal conflicts, heal relationships with themselves and others, and achieve inner peace.

I was seeking inner peace and freedom.

For so long, I did not understand what true freedom was, but I knew I needed to have it. The answer I found… love is freedom. Freedom from ego and all the attachments.

When I reached these moments of freedom, I received the message to write my story.

I was clear, and I could finally hear my calling.

I feel so blessed and grateful for the opportunity.

I look forward to today's events and all that is to come.

I have faith that it will unfold exactly as it is supposed to as I surrender.

I leave you with this simple mantra: the way to erase, erase, erase.

I love you,

I am sorry,

Please forgive me,

Thank you.

Chapter Eleven

What do we do now?

I want to begin this section by acknowledging the profound loss that a man goes through when a baby dies.

It is interesting that I did not ever ask my husband what he was feeling. I must say that I feel bad about that, as I have reflected on it for the purpose of writing this book.

I could beat myself up now and focus on how selfish that was and how it must have been hurtful for him. After all, he had lost his son too.

I will choose to forgive myself and give myself grace that I was much younger, and my pain was all I could handle. I know he forgives me.

I cannot speak to the pain from any position of authority.

I do want to be sure that there is no misunderstanding that when a couple loses a baby, both suffer a significant loss. A loss that is as difficult for the man as the woman in a way that it can only be from the masculine space.

My intention was to focus on my own experience.

My intention is to draw awareness to the wounds of the feminine as her body is experiencing a contradiction to what is happening in her world after the loss of a baby.

We are wounded.

It is important to remember that the loss of a baby does not make you broken. We may feel like an egg cracked on the outside, and there is no hope. Believe me, I understand that feeling.

We are talking about those deep wounds that go straight to the core of who we are—the kind of wound that leaves us feeling broken and lost, unsure of how we will ever heal.

The vulnerability of these wounds can make us feel victimized. Feelings like guilt, despair, blame, fear, apathy, anger, and possibly even hate for the world around us continues without us. The world that does not understand. The world that you want to withdraw from and hide away from.

It is expected to feel this way.

What is essential is to try not to stay here for long.

Our neurology can decide this is our new normal, and we can get stuck in this disempowered, victim place for a long time.

We project this state of being out into the world, and unfortunately, it only brings more back to you.

After a while, it becomes buried in your unconscious mind, and we become less aware of why we feel the way we do.

I am speaking from a place of love. A place from the shared experience of the wounded soul we become. The wounds of our soul begin to spread to the others around us, and the opportunities to love, experience joy and understand others slip away.

We can choose to be empowered by loving ourselves enough to seek support.

I was given the message from the divine that now was the time to tell my story because I had finally reached the place of love, not as a feeling but as a way of showing up in the world.

The ego that is attached to the physical realm of humanness can rise to the spiritual, and that is where we find love at a level where we can shift the consciousness of others.

I have been seeking inner peace and freedom by tapping into my energies and connecting with my soul. This soul work has elevated my spirituality to the level of wanting to encourage women to find their own empowerment and spiritual enlightenment.

Women who have shared this loss experience can support each other in a way no one else can.

Going back to the Old Testament, the women would go out into the fields to have their periods. It is understood that the women began to synchronize their menstrual cycles around the full moon, and they would go to the fields together and provide any needed support to each other.

The women also delivered their babies in the fields. They were each other's midwives, and their powerful stories of their body, soul, and spiritual connections through the events of childbirth and loss inspire us as women today.

Despite the pain and suffering I experienced, the universe is a benevolent place and is on our side. We can heal and we can help others who are where we were to find the mustard seed of faith that will push them one step at a time up that mountain of grief.

We can be the truth that inspires the collective to move away from the pain and toward the present moment and the reality you can create for your future.

Always say "yes" to the present moment.

What could be more futile, more insane, than to create inner resistance to what already is?

What could be more insane than to oppose life itself, which is now and always now?

"Surrender to what is. Say yes to life – and see how life suddenly starts working for you rather than against you." - Eckhart Tolle.

Chapter Twelve

CLOSURE

As I ready myself to write the last chapter of my story, I feel my body tingle with goosebumps.

I have reflected for a while on what to write.

The title says it all. Closure.

Closure brings to my heart so many different emotions. It means repeating goodbye, and that brings so much pain.

Closure means I have stepped into another place of being with my story.

Sometimes, we hang onto the story and the pain of not saying goodbye. I have hung onto my story and kept it in the shadows to keep my son with me.

It was all I knew to do. I did not have a blueprint or a map of how to grieve the loss of a child I never got to know. I never saw his firsts or the person he would have become.

I have spoken of love throughout this story.

The greatest gift I want to leave you with is the love you felt throughout the pain's depths.

We do not feel the depth of this pain without intense love first. I loved this child who was a part of me as much when I said goodbye the first time as if I had known him my whole life.

In the natural path of life, we usually say goodbye to our children when we die.

We love that child for as long as we are alive.

I have loved this child for as long as I have been alive and will love him into the next life, forever and ever. This love far outweighs the pain of the loss.

The greatest gift I want to leave you with is forgiveness.

With love and loss comes a profound and transforming depth of forgiveness. I first had to forgive myself. I wanted to hurt myself as much as the loss of my child was hurting me.

I forgave the doctor because I knew that she did not want this to happen. Her desire to be a doctor says it all. Healing people and bringing new life into this world as her calling says so much about the person she is. Her being a mother to four children says so much about the person she is. By holding her in anger and resentment, I only held myself hostage.

I hope that lessons were learned, and changes were made, and no one would have to endure the outcome we did ever again when it could have been so different.

The greatest gift I want to leave you with is gratitude.

This might be a stretch for many.

Finding gratitude and purpose in the loss of my baby has given me the strength to write this story. I am grateful for the opportunity to bring my story out of the shadows and shed a bright light on the silence imposed on women at a time in their lives when being wrapped in the white light of the divine or whatever you believe in is more important than ever.

I want to illuminate the magnificence of healing when one can trust and feel the understanding and grace of those around one.

I want to illuminate the freedom you will feel when you understand that whatever you feel is exactly what you need to feel.

I want to shed light on the contradictions of the beautiful body, the internal miracles happening because you had a baby, and what is happening in your reality.

I want to illuminate the complexity of this loss and how it will live within you for the rest of your life.

I want you to know that you are not alone.

You are wrapped in the arms of all of us who have experienced this miracle of life and death all in one sweet moment.

You are not alone in the dance of the female body, which is beautiful, wonderful, and painful, all in one sweet moment.

You are not alone in your need to share and find comfort in others; you need to be alone with your intense pain, all in one sweet moment.

You are not alone in feeling guilt, anger, denial, frustration, heart-wrenching pain and the intense moments of love and light all in one sweet moment.

You are not alone in feeling anger towards the people you love the most and need the most in one sweet moment.

You are not alone.

This chapter is about closure, and I will leave the title as it is.

As I write these words from a place of grace, I feel the burning tears running down my cheeks and landing on my breasts where this story began.

My heart is breaking again as I think of the earlier words of saying goodbye.

I cannot say goodbye. I will never say goodbye. We do not have to say goodbye.

I will say until next time, my dearest, darling baby.

Chapter Thirteen

The Gift

Do not stand at my grave and weep.

I am not there. I do not sleep.

I am a thousand winds that blow.

I am the diamond glints on the snow.

I am the sunlight on ripened grain.

I am the gentle autumn rain.

When you awaken in the morning's hush,

I am the swift, uplifting rush.

Of quiet birds in circled flight

I am the soft star that shine at night

Do not stand at my grave and cry.

I am not there. I did not die.

Poem by Mary Elizabeth Frye

It took me a long time to get to this point.

By sharing my story, you will not feel alone and know there is hope.

If you love, forgive and find gratitude in the smallest of things, you will heal and be able to see what I see now.

I see the sparkle in my son's eyes when the sunshine glistens on the water like diamonds.

I feel his soft kisses on my cheeks when the gentle breeze caresses my face.

I hear his voice when the waves lap up against the shoreline with their rhythmical sounds of the water flowing in and back out.

I smell his scent in the fresh rain as it hits the soil.

I feel love when I look into the sky and see a rainbow.

I know I will see him again when I see the sunrise in the morning.

I know the profound peace of whispering his name when I see the sunset in the evening.

I experience the joy of my children in my beloved son, my daughter and my grandsons in this life.

I am more confident than anything else that my son in heaven is at peace and watches over us each day.

He is a part of us in every way, and we are so happy and grateful for that.

Epilogue

Some of the most challenging experiences, such as the loss of a loved one or facing a life-altering situation, are the most intimate.

I've experienced this firsthand, and I understand the depth of emotions that can accompany such moments.

They are the ones that make you hold your breath as you do not know how to breathe out and gather the courage to take the next breath.

These are the ones that inform us the most about who we are and what our purpose on this earth is.

It is revealed when the time is right, and we are ready to accept the truth of our experiences.

I recently read a story about a woman whose adult son was dying.

She shared her story with Oprah Winfrey on the Oprah Show. Oprah spoke about the absolute silence in the studio as this mother shared her truth.

She told how she climbed into bed with her beloved son to spend their last moments together. As he took his last breath, he whispered to his mother. "Mom, it is all so simple. It is all so simple." He closed his eyes, and he died.

This story, shared by Oprah, about a mother's last moments with her dying son, offered me a profound insight. It illuminated a truth that can guide us through life's complexities.

We allow life to get so complicated.

If we ask ourselves how we are making things more complicated, can it support us as we take our next step, even in deep grief?

Love, Forgiveness, and Gratitude are not just words but powerful tools that can simplify our lives and bring us peace even amid chaos.

They can transform our perspective and guide us toward healing and hope.

It can be that simple.

The Wizard of Oz is a beautiful story that was made for children.

My little daughter loved this film and watched the original version repeatedly.

She knew every word of the dialogue and every word of all the songs. She would never sit to watch the movie; instead, she would speak the dialogue, sing the songs, and act out the drama as it unfolded on the TV screen.

She even had a pair of ruby slippers. She would go to bed and fall asleep in them, and her dad and I would have to sneak in and take them off her once she had fallen into a deep slumber.

I read in a book recently that The Wizard of Oz could be considered one of the most excellent spiritual teachings of all time. Oprah Winfrey, 2019.

Reflecting on this comment and the reason why Oprah felt this way, I agree with her one hundred percent.

The yellow brick road represented the pathway to Dorothy's true self.

Along the way, she met the Scarecrow, The Tin Man, and the Cowardly Lion, which could be seen as her disempowered parts. Dorothy believed she needed something outside of herself to discover these parts of herself. The great OZ had all the answers.

The wicked witch presents challenges trying to keep Dorothy from getting her answers and the ruby slippers Dorothy thought she needed to get home.

Glenda the Good Witch helped Dorothy realize she always had the power. She only needed to trust in herself and know she had all she needed right at home.

No matter how far away from home the grief of the loss of a child can take you, you can find your way home. Your ruby slippers, a symbol of your inner strength and resilience, will always carry you back home.

We can feel as Dorothy did alone inside the tornado.

At first, this sense of loss and confusion forces us to seek immediate safety and protection. We soon realize we cannot go back and have no choice but to adapt to the changing landscape. It feels unfamiliar, and the fear of what will come is overwhelming.

No matter how many roadblocks, challenges, heartbreaking moments, anger, resentment, deep grief that feels insurmountable, disappointments, misunderstandings, guilt, and loss, the ruby slippers will take you back to healing and peace.

I wear a mustard seed encased in a little necklace around my neck. Every day, it reminds me that climbing any mountain before me only takes a mustard seed of faith.

I want you to find that mustard seed of faith, hope and belief for better times.

You have this.

I believe in you.

Manufactured by Amazon.ca
Bolton, ON

41382819R00048